THE HORSEMEN OF THE APOCALYPSE

an anthology of poetry to read or not when the world is ending

STEPHEN ROBERT KUTA

Re-invention UK

Copyright
Published by Re-invention UK
Great Leighs
Essex

Copyright © 2020 Stephen Robert Kuta
www.stephenkuta.com

The moral rights of the author have been asserted
Copyright © 2020 Re-invention UK
All Rights Reserved.

No part of this publication may be reproduced, stored in a retrieval system, or transmitted, in any form or by any means, without prior permission in writing of Re-invention UK, or as expressly permitted by law, by licence or under terms agreed with the author.

Cover Image
By Kateryna

Copyright © 2020 Stephen Robert Kuta

FIRST PUBLISHED 2020
ISBN: SOFTCOVER 978-0-9549899-5-8
ISBN: HARDCOVER 978-0-9549899-6-5
DIGITAL VERSION

For Earth

Then I saw a new heaven and a new earth; for the first heaven and the first earth passed away, and there is no longer any sea.

— REVELATION 21:1

THE HORSEMEN OF THE APOCALYPSE

an anthology of poetry to read or not when the world is ending

STEPHEN ROBERT KUTA

Re-invention UK

CONTENTS

Preface	xi
Foreword	xix

PART I
CLASSIC POETRY

1. Fire and Ice	3
2. The Hollow Men	4
3. The Second Coming	9
4. The End of the World	11
5. After Armageddon	12
6. Paradise Lost - Book Twelve	14
7. Paradise Lost - Book Three	16
8. Darkness	17
9. The Raven	21

PART II
MODERN WORKS

10. The Horsemen of the Apocalypse	31
11. The Earth	35
12. Fire and Ice	36
13. The Armageddon	38
14. My Messiah	39
15. Desert Landscapes	41
16. Deep Deep Ocean	43
17. Upon this astral plane	45
18. Sanctuary	47
19. Scream	49

About the Author	51
Also by Stephen Robert Kuta	55

PREFACE

FOUR HORSEMEN OF THE APOCALYPSE

The **Four Horsemen** are figures in Christian theology, appearing in the New Testament's final book, Revelation, an apocalypse written by John of Patmos, as well as in the Old Testament's prophetic Book of Zechariah, and in the Book of Ezekiel, where they are named as punishments from God.

Revelation 6 tells of a book/scroll in God's right hand that is sealed with seven seals. The Lamb of God/Lion of Judah opens the first four of the seven seals, which summons four beings that ride out on white, red, black, and pale horses. To Zechariah, they are described as "the ones whom the Lord has sent to patrol the earth" causing it to rest quietly. Ezekiel lists them as "sword, famine, wild beasts, and plague."

In John's revelation, the first horseman is on a white horse, carrying a bow, and given a crown, riding forward as a figure of Conquest. perhaps invoking Pestilence, Christ, or the Antichrist. The second carries a sword and rides a red horse and is the creator of War. The third is a food merchant riding upon a black horse, symbolising Famine. The fourth and final horse is pale green, and upon it rides Death accompanied by Hades. "They were given authority over a quarter of the earth, to kill with sword, famine, and plague, and by means of the beasts of the earth."

The Christian apocalyptic vision is that the Four Horsemen are to set a divine end time upon the world as harbingers of the Last Judgment. That the number of horsemen is *four* is important: four is the number associated with creation (e.g., the four living creatures) or the earth (e.g., the four winds) in the Book of Revelation. On the significance of fours in Revelation.

WHITE HORSE

Then I saw when the Lamb broke one of the seven seals, and I heard one of the four living creatures saying as with a voice of thunder, "Come." I looked, and behold, a white horse, and he who sat on it had a bow; and a crown was given to him, and he went out conquering and to conquer.
 — Revelation 6:1–2 New American Standard Bible (NASB)
Based on the above passage, a common translation into English is the rider of the White Horse (sometimes referred to as the **White Rider**). He is thought to carry a bow and wear a victor's crown.

RED HORSE

When He broke the second seal, I heard the second living creature saying, "Come." And another, a red horse, went out; and to him who sat on it, it was granted to take peace from Earth, and that men would slay one another; and a great sword was given to him.
 — Revelation 6:3–4 NASB

The rider of the second horse is often taken to represent War (he is often pictured holding a sword upwards as though ready for battle) or mass slaughter. His horse's colour is red (fire); and in some translations, the colour is specifically a "fiery" red. The colour red, as well as the rider's possession of a great sword, suggests blood that is to be spilled. The sword held upward by the second Horseman may represent war or a declaration of war, as seen in heraldry. In military symbolism, swords held upward, especially crossed swords held upward, signify war and entering into battle.

The second Horseman may represent civil war as opposed to the war of conquest that the first Horseman is sometimes said to bring. Other commentators have suggested that it might also represent the persecution of Christians.

BLACK HORSE

When He broke the third seal, I heard the third living creature saying, "Come." I looked, and behold, a black horse; and he who sat on it had a pair of scales in his hand. And I heard something like a voice in the centre of the four living creatures saying, "A quart of wheat for a denarius, and three quarts of barley for a denarius; but do not damage the oil and the wine."

— **Revelation 6:5–6 NASB**

The third Horseman rides a black horse and is popularly understood to be Famine as the Horseman carries a pair of balances or weighing scales, indicating the way that bread would have been weighed during a famine. Other authors interpret the third Horseman as the "Lord as a Law-Giver" holding Scales of Justice. In the passage, it is read that the indicated price of grain is about ten times normal (thus the famine interpretation popularity), with an entire day's wages (a denarius) buying enough wheat for only one person, or enough of the less nutritious barley for three, so that workers would struggle to feed their families.

Of the Four Horsemen, the black horse and its rider are the only ones whose appearance is accompanied by a vocal pronunciation. John hears a voice, unidentified but coming from among the four living creatures, that speaks of the prices of wheat and barley, also saying "and see thou hurt not the oil and the wine". This suggests that the black horse's famine is to drive up the price of grain but leave oil and wine supplies unaffected (though out of reach of the ordinary worker). One explanation for this is that grain crops would have been more naturally susceptible to famine years or locust plagues than olive trees and grapevines, which root more deeply.

The statement might also suggest a continuing abundance of luxuries for the wealthy while staples, such as bread, are scarce, though not totally depleted; such selective scarcity may result from injustice and the deliberate production of luxury crops for the wealthy over grain, as would have happened during the time *Revelation* was written. Alternatively, the preservation of oil and wine could symbolise the preservation of the Christian faithful, who used oil and wine in their sacraments.

PALE HORSE

When the Lamb broke the fourth seal, I heard the voice of the fourth living creature saying, "Come." I looked, and behold, an ashen horse; and he who sat on it had the name Death; and Hades was following with him. Authority was given to them over a fourth of the earth, to kill with sword and with famine and with pestilence and by the wild beasts of the earth.
   — **Revelation 6:7–8 NASB**

The fourth and final Horseman is named Death. Known as "Thanatos", of all the riders, he is the only one to whom the text itself explicitly gives a name. Unlike the other three, he is not described carrying a weapon or other object, instead he is followed by Hades (the resting place of the dead). However, illustrations commonly depict him carrying a scythe (like the Grim Reaper), sword, or other implement.

The colour of Death's horse is written as *khlōros* in the original Koine Greek, which can mean either green/greenish-yellow or pale/pallid. The colour is often translated as "pale", though "ashen", "pale green", and "yellowish green" are other possible interpretations (the Greek word is the root of "chlorophyll" and "chlorine"). Based on uses of the word in ancient Greek medical literature, several scholars suggest that the colour reflects the sickly pallor of a corpse. In some modern artistic depictions, the horse is distinctly green.

The Greek word for plague is θανάτω, which is a variation of Θάνατος, indicating a connection between the Fourth Horseman and plague.

The verse beginning "they were given power over a fourth of the earth" is generally taken as referring to Death and Hades, although some commentators see it as applying to all four horsemen.

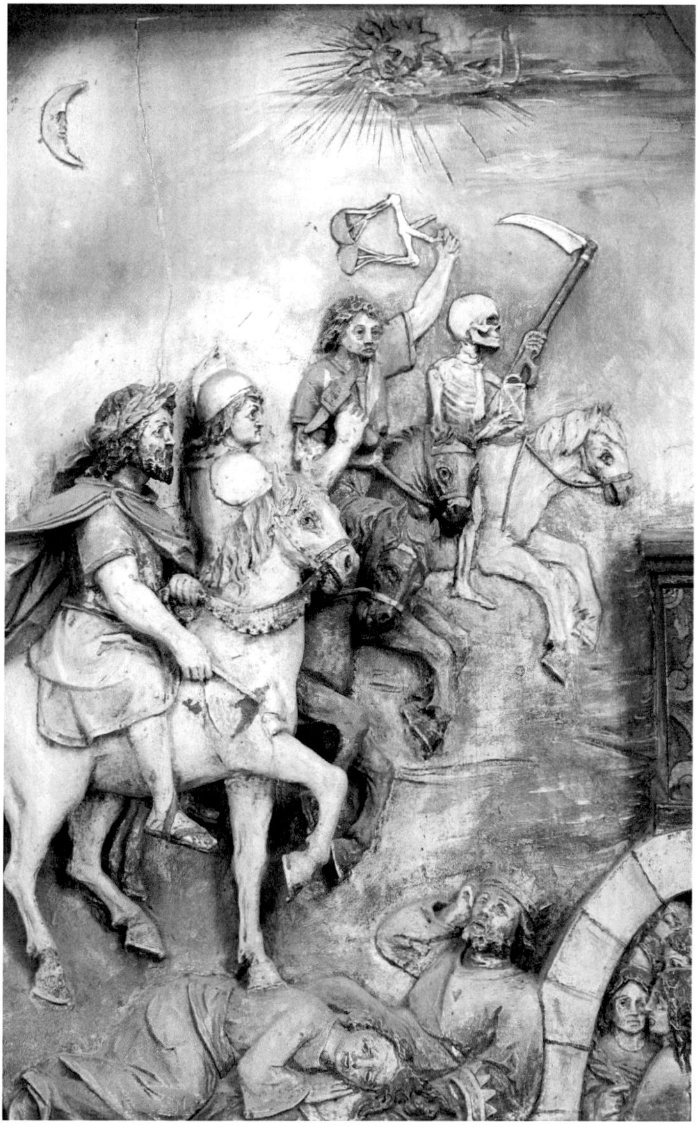

FOREWORD

APOCALYPTIC POETRY, THEN AND NOW

Apocalyptic literature dates all the way to the Hebrew Bible and new testament. Apocalyptic poetry has been a prominent feature of apocalyptic literature, and in the last century, an Apocalypse poetry movement emerged in the UK, with many esteemed poets of the time contributing.

Even eternal optimists can concede that there is currently a degree of gloom and dread around. And so now seems like an apt time to share some of my favourite apocalyptic poetry from down the years, and also pick out some new works. With roots in mythology, nightmare and war, I think you will agree that these are some of the most powerful poems you will come across.

T.S. ELIOT - THE HOLLOW MEN

In 1925, T.S Eliot gave us The Hollow Men. The men described in the poem seem trapped in another world which exists between life and death - a kind of void in the middle of darkness and light. In the same vein as another of Eliot's most famous poems - 'The Waste Land' - The Hollow Men describes lost souls, creating a haunting mood through repetition; repeating the ominous line 'This is the way the world ends' three times towards the end of the poem. Large parts of the poem - 'here we go around the prickly pear', for instance - are open to interpretation, but the dark sense of all being lost is not.

ARCHIBALD MACLEISH - THE END OF THE WORLD

In 'The End of the World', MacLeish surprises and even stuns with his sudden switch between describing characters who are part of the circus and utter oblivion. The colon positioned at the end of the first octave, 'quite unexpectedly the top blew off:' sets the scene for an alarming second part of the poem, 'There in the sudden blackness, the black pall. Of nothing - nothing, nothing, nothing at all'. From the lively happenings under the big top to the top blowing open, and what seems like, well, the end of the world, MacLeish was able to create confusion, shock and doom in a poetic 'bait and switch'.

CZESŁAW MIŁOSZ - A SONG FOR THE END OF THE WORLD

Czesław Miłosz, the winner of the Nobel Peace Prize for Literature in 1980, begins this poem describing a scene of serenity with bees flying, fisherman mending their nets and women walking through fields. Indeed throughout the poem, there seems to be a lack of urgency; a lack of realisation that this is in fact the end of the world. Even up until the last stanza, the 'white-haired old man' or 'would-be prophet' described is going about his business 'for he's much too busy', but the last three lines reveal a dark, conclusive truth; 'Repeats while he binds his tomatoes: / There will be no other end of the world. / There will be no other end of the world'.

RICHARD WILBUR - ADVICE TO A PROPHET

Written in 1961, Advice to a Prophet is another poem which could chime with today's society as we face up to a formidable challenge. It asks people looking ahead to the potential destruction of the world not to mourn the loss of people, but to consider what people will be like without the world. As the name of the poem suggests, this advice is given directly to 'the prophet'. The poem can act as a warning against complacency and self-centredness which humans can be prone to, especially in times which could be considered approaching apocalyptic.

JOY HARJO - PERHAPS THE WORLD ENDS HERE

For those of us dealing with the daily monotony of lockdown, Joy Harjo offers some food for thought - no pun intended - with 'Perhaps the World Ends Here'. The poem starts: 'The world begins at a kitchen table. No matter what, we must eat to live.' This might ring true with many whose major adventure during the corona virus outbreak and worldwide lockdown had become a trip to the supermarket and back. Her final message seems to be one of hope and humour in the face of a harsh reality: 'Perhaps the world will end at the kitchen table, while we are laughing and crying, eating off the last sweet bite.'

This anthology of poetry, The Horseman of the Apocalypse',

has been broken down into two parts, a collected anthology of nine classic poems and ten new works from my own personal collection. The title piece has had overwhelming response on social media and has been liked 36,600 times on facebook and 43,730 times on Instagram. An excerpt from this poem is below and the full published poem can be found in part two of this collection.

The world fell into darkness, cataclysm exploded, across the starry night
    The moon a distant beacon, a path of guiding light.
    The grey and barren roads stretch across the hill
    And the trumpets came sounding, sounding
    As the horseman appeared in sight.

❧ I ❧
CLASSIC POETRY

I

FIRE AND ICE

ROBERT FROST

"**Fire and Ice**" is one of Robert Frost's most popular poems. It was published in December 1920 in *Harper's Magazine* and in 1923 in his Pulitzer Prize-winning book *New Hampshire*. It discusses the end of the world, likening the elemental force of fire with the emotion of desire, and ice with hate. It is one of Frost's best-known and most anthologised poems.

Some say the world will end in fire,
    Some say in ice.
    From what I've tasted of desire
I hold with those who favour fire.
But if it had to perish twice,
I think I know enough of hate
To say that for destruction ice
Is also great
And would suffice.

2
THE HOLLOW MEN
THOMAS STEARNS ELIOT

"**The Hollow Men**" (1925) is a poem by T. S. Eliot. Its themes are, like those of many of Eliot's poems, overlapping and fragmentary, but it is recognised to be concerned most with post–World War I Europe under the Treaty of Versailles (which Eliot despised), the difficulty of hope and religious conversion, and, as some critics argue, Eliot's own failed marriage (Vivienne Haigh-Wood Eliot might have been having an affair with Bertrand Russell). The poem is divided into five parts and consists of 98 lines of which the last four are "probably the most quoted lines of any 20th-century poet writing in English".

Mistah Kurtz-he dead
        A penny for the Old Guy

I

. . .

WE ARE THE HOLLOW MEN
    We are the stuffed men
    Leaning together
    Headpiece filled with straw. Alas!
    Our dried voices, when
    We whisper together
    Are quiet and meaningless
    As wind in dry grass
    Or rats' feet over broken glass
    In our dry cellar

    Shape without form, shade without colour,
    Paralysed force, gesture without motion;

    Those who have crossed
    With direct eyes, to death's other Kingdom
    Remember us-if at all-not as lost
    Violent souls, but only
    As the hollow men
    The stuffed men.

II

EYES I DARE NOT MEET IN DREAMS
    In death's dream kingdom
    These do not appear:
    There, the eyes are
    Sunlight on a broken column
    There, is a tree swinging

And voices are
In the wind's singing
More distant and more solemn
Than a fading star.

Let me be no nearer
In death's dream kingdom
Let me also wear
Such deliberate disguises
Rat's coat, crowskin, crossed staves
In a field
Behaving as the wind behaves
No nearer-

Not that final meeting
In the twilight kingdom

III

THIS IS THE DEAD LAND
This is cactus land
Here the stone images
Are raised, here they receive
The supplication of a dead man's hand
Under the twinkle of a fading star.

Is it like this
In death's other kingdom
Waking alone
At the hour when we are
Trembling with tenderness

IV

THE EYES ARE NOT HERE
   There are no eyes here
   In this valley of dying stars
   In this hollow valley
   This broken jaw of our lost kingdoms

   In this last of meeting places
   We grope together
   And avoid speech
   Gathered on this beach of the tumid river

   Sightless, unless
   The eyes reappear
   As the perpetual star
   Multifoliate rose
   Of death's twilight kingdom
   The hope only
   Of empty men.

V

HERE WE GO ROUND THE PRICKLY PEAR
   Prickly pear prickly pear

Here we go round the prickly pear
At five o'clock in the morning.

Between the idea
And the reality
Between the motion
And the act
Falls the Shadow
                      For Thine is the Kingdom

Between the conception
And the creation
Between the emotion
And the response
Falls the Shadow
                      Life is very long

Between the desire
And the spasm
Between the potency
And the existence
Between the essence
And the descent
Falls the Shadow
                      For Thine is the Kingdom

For Thine is
Life is
For Thine is the

This is the way the world ends
This is the way the world ends
This is the way the world ends
Not with a bang but a whimper.

THE SECOND COMING

WILLIAM BUTLER YEATS

"**The Second Coming**" is a poem written by Irish poet W. B. Yeats in 1919, first printed in *The Dial* in November 1920, and afterwards included in his 1921 collection of verses *Michael Robartes and the Dancer*. The poem uses Christian imagery regarding the Apocalypse and Second Coming to allegorically describe the atmosphere of post-war Europe. It is considered a major work of modernist poetry and has been reprinted in several collections, including *The Norton Anthology of Modern Poetry*.

Turning and turning in the widening gyre
    The falcon cannot hear the falconer;
    Things fall apart; the centre cannot hold;
Mere anarchy is loosed upon the world,
The blood-dimmed tide is loosed, and everywhere
The ceremony of innocence is drowned;
The best lack all conviction, while the worst
Are full of passionate intensity.

. . .

Surely some revelation is at hand;
    Surely the Second Coming is at hand.
    The Second Coming! Hardly are those words out
    When a vast image out of *Spiritus Mundi*
    Troubles my sight: somewhere in sands of the desert
    A shape with lion body and the head of a man,
    A gaze blank and pitiless as the sun,
    Is moving its slow thighs, while all about it
    Reel shadows of the indignant desert birds.
    The darkness drops again; but now I know
    That twenty centuries of stony sleep
    Were vexed to nightmare by a rocking cradle,
    And what rough beast, its hour come round at last,
    Slouches towards Bethlehem to be born?

4

THE END OF THE WORLD

ARCHIBALD MACLEISH

Quite unexpectedly, as Vasserot
      The armless ambidextrian was lighting
      A match between his great and second toe,
And Ralph the lion was engaged in biting
The neck of Madame Sossman while the drum
Pointed, and Teeny was about to cough
In waltz-time swinging Jocko by the thumb
Quite unexpectedly to top blew off:

AND THERE, THERE OVERHEAD, THERE, THERE HUNG OVER
    Those thousands of white faces, those dazed eyes,
    There in the starless dark, the poise, the hover,
    There with vast wings across the cancelled skies,
    There in the sudden blackness the black pall
    Of nothing, nothing, nothing — nothing at all.

AFTER ARMAGEDDON

CLARK ASHTON SMITH

God walks lightly in the gardens of a cold, dark star,
   Knowing not the dust that gathers in His garments' fold;
God signs Him with the clay, marks Him with the mould,
Walking in the fields unsunned of a sad, lost war,
In a star long cold.

God treads brightly where the bones of unknown things lie,
   Pale with His splendour as the frost in a moon-bleached place;
   God sees the tombs by the light of His face,
   He shudders at the runes writ thereon, and His shadow on the sky
   Shudders hugely in space.

God talks briefly with His armies of the tomb-born worm,

God holds parley with the grey worm and pale, avid moth:
Their mouths have eaten all, but the worm is wroth
With a dark hunger still, and he murmurs harm
With the murmuring moth.

God turns Him heavenward in haste from a death-dark star,

But His robes are assoilèd by the dust of unknown things dead;

The grey worm follows creeping, and the pale moth has fed

Couched in a secret golden fold of His broad-trained cimar

Like a doom unsaid.

❧ 6 ☙
PARADISE LOST - BOOK TWELVE
JOHN MILTON

Paradise Lost is an epic poem in blank verse by the 17th-century English poet John Milton (1608–1674). The first version, published in 1667, consists of ten books with over ten thousand lines of verse. A second edition followed in 1674, arranged into twelve books (in the manner of Virgil's *Aeneid*) with minor revisions throughout. It is considered by critics to be Milton's major work, and it helped solidify his reputation as one of the greatest English poets of his time.

The poem concerns the biblical story of the Fall of Man: the temptation of Adam and Eve by the fallen angel Satan and their expulsion from the Garden of Eden. Milton's purpose, stated in Book I, is to "justify the ways of God to men.

THE HORSEMEN OF THE APOCALYPSE

With glory and power to judge both quick and dead [460]
To judge th' unfaithful dead, but to reward
His faithful, and receave them into bliss,
Whether in Heav'n or Earth, for then the Earth
Shall all be Paradise, far happier place
Then this of *Eden*, and far happier daies. [465]

❧ 7 ☙

PARADISE LOST - BOOK THREE
JOHN MILTON

The World shall burn, and from her ashes spring
New Heav'n and Earth, wherein the just shall dwell [335]
And after all thir tribulations long
See golden days, fruitful of golden deeds,
With Joy and Love triumphing, and fair Truth.
Then thou thy regal Scepter shalt lay by,
For regal Scepter then no more shall need, [340]
God shall be All in All. But all ye Gods,
Adore him, who to compass all this dies,
Adore the Son, and honour him as mee.

8

DARKNESS

LORD BYRON (GEORGE GORDON)

"**Darkness**" is a poem written by Lord Byron in July 1816. That year was known as the Year Without a Summer, because Mount Tambora had erupted in the Dutch East Indies the previous year, casting enough sulphur into the atmosphere to reduce global temperatures and cause abnormal weather across much of north-east America and northern Europe. This pall of darkness inspired Byron to write his poem. Literary critics were initially content to classify it as a "last man" poem, telling the apocalyptic story of the last man on earth. More recent critics have focused on the poem's historical context, as well as the anti-biblical nature of the poem, despite its many references to the Bible. The poem was written only months after the end of Byron's marriage to Anne Isabella Milbanke.

I had a dream, which was not all a dream.
    The bright sun was extinguish'd, and the stars
    Did wander darkling in the eternal space,
Rayless, and pathless, and the icy earth
Swung blind and blackening in the moonless air;

Morn came and went—and came, and brought no day,
And men forgot their passions in the dread
Of this their desolation; and all hearts
Were chill'd into a selfish prayer for light:
And they did live by watchfires—and the thrones,
The palaces of crowned kings—the huts,
The habitations of all things which dwell,
Were burnt for beacons; cities were consum'd,
And men were gather'd round their blazing homes
To look once more into each other's face;
Happy were those who dwelt within the eye
Of the volcanos, and their mountain-torch:
A fearful hope was all the world contain'd;
Forests were set on fire—but hour by hour
They fell and faded—and the crackling trunks
Extinguish'd with a crash—and all was black.
The brows of men by the despairing light
Wore an unearthly aspect, as by fits
The flashes fell upon them; some lay down
And hid their eyes and wept; and some did rest
Their chins upon their clenched hands, and smil'd;
And others hurried to and fro, and fed
Their funeral piles with fuel, and look'd up
With mad disquietude on the dull sky,
The pall of a past world; and then again
With curses cast them down upon the dust,
And gnash'd their teeth and howl'd: the wild birds shriek'd
And, terrified, did flutter on the ground,
And flap their useless wings; the wildest brutes
Came tame and tremulous; and vipers crawl'd
And twin'd themselves among the multitude,
Hissing, but stingless—they were slain for food.
And War, which for a moment was no more,
Did glut himself again: a meal was bought

With blood, and each sate sullenly apart
Gorging himself in gloom: no love was left;
All earth was but one thought—and that was death
Immediate and inglorious; and the pang
Of famine fed upon all entrails—men
Died, and their bones were tombless as their flesh;
The meagre by the meagre were devour'd,
Even dogs assail'd their masters, all save one,
And he was faithful to a corse, and kept
The birds and beasts and famish'd men at bay,
Till hunger clung them, or the dropping dead
Lur'd their lank jaws; himself sought out no food,
But with a piteous and perpetual moan,
And a quick desolate cry, licking the hand
Which answer'd not with a caress—he died.
The crowd was famish'd by degrees; but two
Of an enormous city did survive,
And they were enemies: they met beside
The dying embers of an altar-place
Where had been heap'd a mass of holy things
For an unholy usage; they rak'd up,
And shivering scrap'd with their cold skeleton hands
The feeble ashes, and their feeble breath
Blew for a little life, and made a flame
Which was a mockery; then they lifted up
Their eyes as it grew lighter, and beheld
Each other's aspects—saw, and shriek'd, and died—
Even of their mutual hideousness they died,
Unknowing who he was upon whose brow
Famine had written Fiend. The world was void,
The populous and the powerful was a lump,
Seasonless, herbless, treeless, manless, lifeless—
A lump of death—a chaos of hard clay.
The rivers, lakes and ocean all stood still,

And nothing stirr'd within their silent depths;
Ships sailorless lay rotting on the sea,
And their masts fell down piecemeal: as they dropp'd
They slept on the abyss without a surge—
The waves were dead; the tides were in their grave,
The moon, their mistress, had expir'd before;
The winds were wither'd in the stagnant air,
And the clouds perish'd; Darkness had no need
Of aid from them—She was the Universe.

9

THE RAVEN

EDGAR ALLAN POE

The Raven‖ poem by Edgar Allan Poe contains three types of archetype imagery, they are apocalyptic, demonic, and analogical imagery (analogy of innocence and analogy of experience). This poem also contains the four types of cyclical symbolism of archetype, they are divine world, human world, animal world, and mineral world. It is also found that this poem has a structure of sparagmos due to the dark myth and the confusion world that cover the theme of poem. Finally, this poem is divided into six phases of winter which is related to the literary genre of irony and satire that explain more about the sorrowfulness of the author, Edgar Allan Poe because his lover, Lenore leaves him.

Once upon a midnight dreary, while I pondered, weak and weary,
Over many a quaint and curious volume of forgotten lore—

While I nodded, nearly napping, suddenly there came a tapping,
As of some one gently rapping, rapping at my chamber door.
"'Tis some visitor," I muttered, "tapping at my chamber door—
Only this and nothing more."

AH, DISTINCTLY I REMEMBER IT WAS IN THE BLEAK December;
And each separate dying ember wrought its ghost upon the floor.
Eagerly I wished the morrow;—vainly I had sought to borrow
From my books surcease of sorrow—sorrow for the lost Lenore—
For the rare and radiant maiden whom the angels name Lenore—
Nameless *here* for evermore.

AND THE SILKEN, SAD, UNCERTAIN RUSTLING OF EACH purple curtain
Thrilled me—filled me with fantastic terrors never felt before;
So that now, to still the beating of my heart, I stood repeating
"'Tis some visitor entreating entrance at my chamber door—
Some late visitor entreating entrance at my chamber door;—
This it is and nothing more."

. . .

Presently my soul grew stronger; hesitating then no longer,
 "Sir," said I, "or Madam, truly your forgiveness I implore;
 But the fact is I was napping, and so gently you came rapping,
 And so faintly you came tapping, tapping at my chamber door,
 That I scarce was sure I heard you"—here I opened wide the door;—
 Darkness there and nothing more.

Deep into that darkness peering, long I stood there wondering, fearing,
 Doubting, dreaming dreams no mortal ever dared to dream before;
 But the silence was unbroken, and the stillness gave no token,
 And the only word there spoken was the whispered word, "Lenore?"
 This I whispered, and an echo murmured back the word, "Lenore!"—
 Merely this and nothing more.

Back into the chamber turning, all my soul within me burning,
 Soon again I heard a tapping somewhat louder than before.
 "Surely," said I, "surely that is something at my window lattice;
 Let me see, then, what thereat is, and this mystery explore—

Let my heart be still a moment and this mystery explore;—

    'Tis the wind and nothing more!"

Open here I flung the shutter, when, with many a flirt and flutter,

In there stepped a stately Raven of the saintly days of yore;

    Not the least obeisance made he; not a minute stopped or stayed he;

    But, with mien of lord or lady, perched above my chamber door—

Perched upon a bust of Pallas just above my chamber door—

    Perched, and sat, and nothing more.

Then this ebony bird beguiling my sad fancy into smiling,

By the grave and stern decorum of the countenance it wore,

"Though thy crest be shorn and shaven, thou," I said, "art sure no craven,

Ghastly grim and ancient Raven wandering from the Nightly shore—

Tell me what thy lordly name is on the Night's Plutonian shore!"

    Quoth the Raven "Nevermore."

    Much I marvelled this ungainly fowl to hear discourse so plainly,

Though its answer little meaning—little relevancy bore;

For we cannot help agreeing that no living human being
  Ever yet was blessed with seeing bird above his chamber door—
Bird or beast upon the sculptured bust above his chamber door,
  With such name as "Nevermore."

But the Raven, sitting lonely on the placid bust, spoke only
That one word, as if his soul in that one word he did outpour.
  Nothing farther then he uttered—not a feather then he fluttered—
Till I scarcely more than muttered "Other friends have flown before—
On the morrow *he* will leave me, as my Hopes have flown before."
  Then the bird said "Nevermore."

Startled at the stillness broken by reply so aptly spoken,
"Doubtless," said I, "what it utters is its only stock and store
  Caught from some unhappy master whom unmerciful Disaster
  Followed fast and followed faster till his songs one burden bore—
Till the dirges of his Hope that melancholy burden bore
  Of 'Never—nevermore'."

  . . .

But the Raven still beguiling all my fancy into smiling,
Straight I wheeled a cushioned seat in front of bird, and bust and door;
Then, upon the velvet sinking, I betook myself to linking
Fancy unto fancy, thinking what this ominous bird of yore—
What this grim, ungainly, ghastly, gaunt, and ominous bird of yore
Meant in croaking "Nevermore."

This I sat engaged in guessing, but no syllable expressing
To the fowl whose fiery eyes now burned into my bosom's core;
This and more I sat divining, with my head at ease reclining
On the cushion's velvet lining that the lamp-light gloated o'er,
But whose velvet-violet lining with the lamp-light gloating o'er,
She shall press, ah, nevermore!

Then, methought, the air grew denser, perfumed from an unseen censer
Swung by Seraphim whose foot-falls tinkled on the tufted floor.
"Wretch," I cried, "thy God hath lent thee—by these angels he hath sent thee
Respite—respite and nepenthe from thy memories of Lenore;

Quaff, oh quaff this kind nepenthe and forget this lost Lenore!"

Quoth the Raven "Nevermore."

"Prophet!" said I, "thing of evil!—prophet still, if bird or devil!—

Whether Tempter sent, or whether tempest tossed thee here ashore,

Desolate yet all undaunted, on this desert land enchanted—

On this home by Horror haunted—tell me truly, I implore—

Is there—*is* there balm in Gilead?—tell me—tell me, I implore!"

Quoth the Raven "Nevermore."

"Prophet!" said I, "thing of evil!—prophet still, if bird or devil!

By that Heaven that bends above us—by that God we both adore—

Tell this soul with sorrow laden if, within the distant Aidenn,

It shall clasp a sainted maiden whom the angels name Lenore—

Clasp a rare and radiant maiden whom the angels name Lenore."

Quoth the Raven "Nevermore."

"Be that word our sign of parting, bird or fiend!" I shrieked, upstarting—

"Get thee back into the tempest and the Night's Plutonian shore!

Leave no black plume as a token of that lie thy soul hath spoken!

Leave my loneliness unbroken!—quit the bust above my door!

Take thy beak from out my heart, and take thy form from off my door!"

Quoth the Raven "Nevermore."

AND THE RAVEN, NEVER FLITTING, STILL IS sitting, *still* is sitting

On the pallid bust of Pallas just above my chamber door;

And his eyes have all the seeming of a demon's that is dreaming,

And the lamp-light o'er him streaming throws his shadow on the floor;

And my soul from out that shadow that lies floating on the floor

Shall be lifted—nevermore!

❧ II ☙
MODERN WORKS

By Stephen Robert Kuta

10

THE HORSEMEN OF THE APOCALYPSE

A BIBLICAL TALE

The world fell into darkness, cataclysm exploded, across the starry night
The moon a distant beacon, a path of guiding light.
The grey and barren roads stretch across the hill
And the trumpets came sounding, sounding
As the horseman appeared in sight.

At first appeared a white rider, proud and stern was he
   A crown upon his forehead with a bow we all could see.
   His cloak was blood red and velvet and shimmered with sparkly hue
   His voice was full of thunder, loud and deep with thunder
   His eyes a ghostly blue.

Everyday we heard it, a message loud and clear
   It filled our lives with worry, and spread a plague of fear.
   Some took all and plenty and filled their cupboards full
   Leaving the weak and helpless with very little all
   And so the horseman came a riding, riding towards the city wall.

Then appeared a second rider, on a horse of fiery red
   Clasped in hand a metal hilt, a symbol of his stead.
   He wore with pride a coat, of Ireland emerald green
   The hooves of his horse came crashing, and broke the bones of the weak.
   With a blade so sharp it cut us down and the Earth did fall and shriek.

For the Earth we whipped and did not care
   For the Earth we did not share.
   We used and abused for shameful gain
   We hurt and yes we hated, hated
   Hurt and yes we hated upon our Earth so fare.

. . .

THE HORSEMEN OF THE APOCALYPSE

And so rode in the scales of justice, A man seated upon a horse of black.
He brought a wake of famine,
And the weight of the Earth on his back.
We wept with little dignity as those we love did fall
A punishment for hatred, he cast upon us all.

The world fell into darkness, The moon a distant light
Grey and barren roads lay empty, the Earth a ghastly sight.
It came and took and spread like fire
As the trumpets continued sounding, calling
The horseman through the night.

Than the fourth and final horseman came, dressed in black like death
He placed his hands around the Earth and it chocked its final breath.
His horse was pale and ashen,
Death in the morning light
The horseman came a-riding, riding, the horseman did come riding
Upon a stormy night.

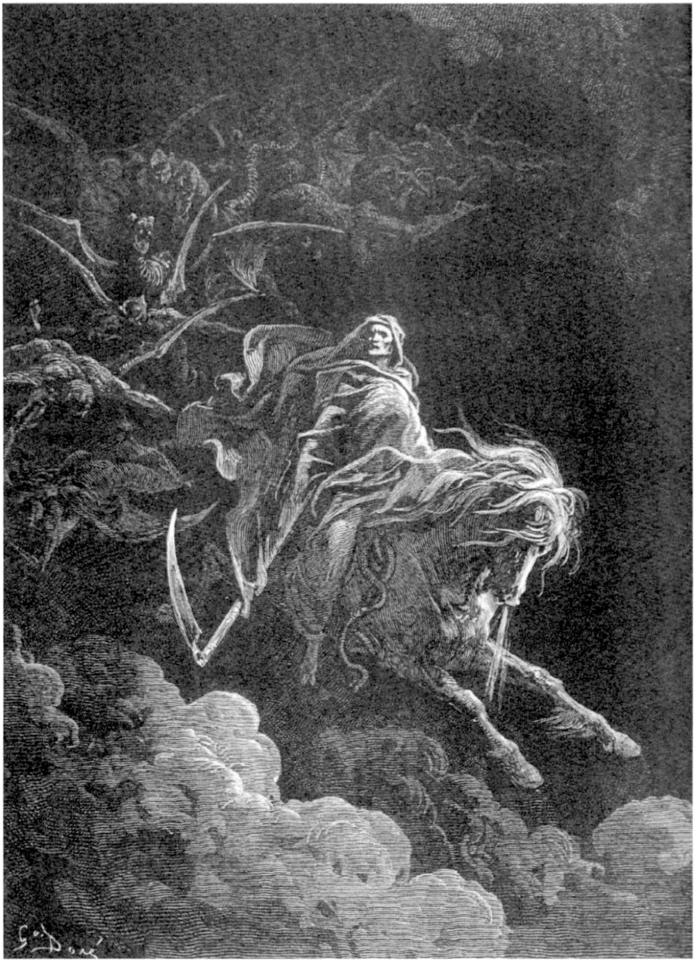

11
THE EARTH

The Earth
    Has stopped spinning
    And the sky burns red
Across the horizon.
This road I stand upon is empty
Twisted metal
Scattered across the ruins.
In this emptiness
I am alone
Alone as I was
When the world was full.

12

FIRE AND ICE

ROMANTICISM IN AN APOCALYPTIC WORLD

If the world did end in fire
    Or as cold as winter ice
    Let the love inside, inspire
Not the hatred, forfeit it's price
Live your life.
What you require
Let your world suffice
Allow your heart, what you desire
Be mistaken...
once...
Or twice

LET OTHERS ASPIRE.
    As so too. You live.

THE HORSEMEN OF THE APOCALYPSE

13
THE ARMAGEDDON

Through the centuries of mankind
    through the corridors of mans mind.
    There are passages written, in ink and blood
History buried, beneath soil and mud.

There comes a time in history
    When prophesy opens its book of mystery.
    The lord of darkness rises forth
    To conquer all south, east, west and north.

A battle dividing heaven and hell
    Souls to old nick, the devil quell.

🕊 14 🕊

MY MESSIAH

Out of my window
      Into the fog I see,
      A blanket of sorrow
I hear the birds call to me.
I can't see through the mist
The grey blinds my way,
Birds fill the sky
They cry today.

I PULL AWAY FROM MY BODY
    My silk woven sheet,
    And step upon the water
    Upon my own two feet.
    The lands are flooding,
    The sky's are grey,
    The birds song does call
    Me far away.

            . . .

I FOLLOW, THE WORDS
　Which beckon me,
　Out of Earth,
　Out of sea.
　My messiah is calling
　He awaits me in vain,
　He is to heal this Earth,
　Take away its pain.

I AWAIT FOR HIM,
　To wash away the tears that flood,
　To clear away the blanket of fog,
　To bury our sorrow, away in the mud.
　To bring out the sunshine,
　Prevent the birds from crying,
　To heal our wars,
　Send the angels flying.
　To end all violence,
　To watch the children play,
　When that happens, My Messiah
　It will be a glorious day.

15
DESERT LANDSCAPES

Lands that once flourished, green and alive
    A savannah of plenty where animals thrive.
    Grazing gazelle, lion cubs at play
Hippos bathing and lying in clay.

Life in abundance, free and wild
    Food of plenty, weather so mild.
    Catastrophic consequences, the dry season is here
Mother Nature strikes, vultures appear.

The savannah is dying, water holes dry
    Alligators and crocodiles all begin to die.
    Dehydration and hunger, both takes its toll
Danger lurks, in the waters hole.

Buried in dust the carcasses of the dead
    Noises in the distance of the stampedes tread.

Animals of the savannah, live a hard life
In danger of so much, man takes their life.

ACROSS THE PLAINS, BLACK WITH DEATH
The savannah dies, and takes its last breath.
Danger and death in so many shapes
Look at the savannah, and desert landscapes.

16

DEEP DEEP OCEAN

Deep deep ocean, listen well
    To your great roaring mass
    And its gentle swell.
Listen to the gulls, hear their cries
Hear the great whale
Which brings water to my eyes.

Deep deep ocean, you are a great mystery
    A killing field for man
    With pages of history.
    That colour blue, to instantly red
    The killing harpooner
    And the whales are dead.

Deep deep ocean, a great abyss
    A haunted world of harmony
    I could not miss.
    A formidable encounter, with stories foretold

Stories of a sea monster
Sunken ships and buried gold.

Deep deep ocean, how dead calm tonight
A rubbish dump for humans
Where the sun cast dunes of light.
That colour blue, turned black or red
A harpoon, an oil tanker
And then the sea is dead.

Deep deep ocean, a changing season
Your vast expanse
Exploited without reason.
Deep deep ocean, and the bottom of the sea bed
In the arms of unconsciousness
And the dying and the dead.,
With all my sorrow and pain
I will remember and think of you in vain.

17

UPON THIS ASTRAL PLANE

FROM THE ANTHOLOGY - PAINT THE SKY
WITH STARS (IN REMEMBRANCE TO THE
BOXING DAY TSUNAMI 2004)

Planet Earth, Planet Earth listen to me
    Quieten this storm, from the Earth, Wind and Sea.
Hear us in memory, hear us in voice
Blanket our loss, silence this noise.

But not without sincerity, not without care,
    Remember the living, whom passed from us out there.
    Remember our hearts, are all but the same
    Upon our union, human by name.

Planet Earth, Planet Earth did you hear those that cried
    Are you aware of our loss, all the people who died,
    Hear us in memory, please hear us in voice
    Gentle in composure, gentle in poise.

. . .

With all your sincerity, show us you care
Remember the living, who lost love ones out there.
Remember our hearts, are all human, but the same
And you are our planet, Earth by name.

So it is, upon our Astral Plane
And so upon this world,
I answer, I whisper, and I let my words unfold
I shall remember and forever care... the day the world took hold.
26th December 2004

18
SANCTUARY

Safe in my sanctuary
    Hidden away from darkness.

SAFE IN MY SANCTUARY
    Hidden away from the world.

SAFE IN MY SANCTUM
    This my holy shrine.

SAFE IN MY SANCTUM
    Not to be profound.

YOU ARE MY SACREDNESS
    My love so true.

You are my sacredness
Till the very end.

SAFE IN MY SANCTUARY
    Free from chaos.

SAFE IN MY SANCTUARY
    Safe in my sanctum
    You are my sacredness.

19
SCREAM

How many things make me scream
　　A horrible nightmare, a terrifying dream.
　　An ocean of death, black blood flows free
Damaged oil tankers, ruin the sea.

RAINFORESTS ONCE PLENTY, NOW ASH AND DUST
　　Destroyed by greed, greed and lust.
　　Famine and hunger, death despair
　　in a polluted planet, chocking the air.

ABOUT THE AUTHOR

Stephen Robert Kuta was born in Chelmsford, Essex, England in 1978, the second eldest of five children, he is of second-generation Polish/English descent. His grandfather spent his young adult life in a Nazi Labour Camp before arriving in England in the early 1950's. Stephen studied English Language, Literature, History and Drama and continues to study humanities pushing his learning in his fields of interest. Stephen went onto to publish prose and poetry in selected anthologies throughout the 1990's and was credited with a publication in the national newspaper, the Sunday Mirror in remembrance of Diana Princess of Wales. He eventually edited an anthology of work in 2005, a book intended to bring the voices of the world together collectively in response to the 2004 Boxing Day Tsunami. The book was of a limited run and all profits from its sale were donated to the Tsunami Earthquake Fund. The book has gone onto become a valued piece of social history and often used in university academic studies. The book now sells for high values. Stephen continues to push boundaries in humanities and creative writing, spending much of his time managing various historical and personal blogs online all of which have been met with praise and popularity. Humanities have always been at the forefront of his interests, and he has continued learning with the open university focusing on the great war historically and through study with wartime literature and poetry. Genealogy is also one of his key interests and one of his biggest drives in future publications. His families past has always intrigued him and he developed an interest and love of history from a very early age, as young as 8 years old he was reading books about the history of England and his imagination about the past grew from there. He began studying Genealogy aged 18 and has continued to research his family history since 1997, he is ever grateful to his great-grandmother Doris, grandfather William and his father for the support and help they gave when he first began his journey into his families' past. he has since developed an interest in Palaeography and has transcribed many records of probate dating from the early 16th century. Besides Humanities Stephen also has a keen interest in Modelling, Photography, Art and dramatics he has been featured in Model Citizen Magazine and photographed by Men Art, his collected photography portfolio was published in 2018 in the book 'My Life in Pictures.

S.R. Kuta lives in Great Leighs, Essex with his niece Yhana.

[f] [t] [o]

BY THE SAME AUTHOR

Anthologies

Paint the Sky with Stars (In remembrance to the Boxing Day Tsunami 2004)

Once I Write of Love (Selected Poetry and Prose)

War and Verse (Poetry and prose from World War One, as seen in the National Press)

Life in Monochrome (Poetry and Prose)

The Horsemen of the Apocalypse (an anthology of poetry to read or not when the world is ending)

History and Biography

Mrs Mary Plaskett (1739 - 1827)

Selina's Letter (Tales of Suicide from Victorian and Edwardian London)

Semper Fidelis (The Lwów Eaglets)

For God's sake hold your tongue, and let me love (Biography and Select Poetry of John Donne)

The Devil's Servant (The Dark Conjurer of Batcombe)

Stormforge Saga

Stormforge (Lightning Strikes on Seadragon wings) - Book One (The Jarl of Møre)

Stormforge (Lightning Strikes on Seadragon wings) - Book Two (The Duke of Normandy)

Milton Keynes UK
Ingram Content Group UK Ltd.
UKRC030009090724
445210UK00004B/12